SUPERTATO

STICKER ACTIVITY

This book belongs to

EVIL PEA

Based on the Supertato picture books
by Sue Hendra & Paul Linnet

SIMON & SCHUSTER

London New York Sydney Toronto New Delhi

Sticker Dress-Up

Supertato and his friends are getting ready for the Supermarket Carnival. Can you use your stickers to dress them up in colourful costumes?

Happy Birthday, Supertato!

Use your stickers to add some delicious
decorations to Supertato's birthday cake!

Spot the Difference

Can you spot the six differences
between image A and image B?

Cape Makeover

Using your stickers, give Supertato's famous cape a fresh new look!
Make sure The Evil Pea doesn't write anything rude . . .

Evil Pea Takeover!

Uh-oh – it looks like our hero's in trouble! Cover Supertato in as many Evil Pea stickers as you can.

Supertato thinks he's so smart, but he's no match for my army of peas. **Peas, attack!**

Super Veggies in Disguise

The Super Veggies are going undercover on a top-secret mission.
Use your stickers to give each veggie a clever disguise.

Spot the Difference

Can you spot the five differences
between image A and image B?

A

B

Hide-and-Seek

Supertato and his friends are playing hide-and-seek!
Can you help Supertato through the maze to where Broccoli is hiding?

Run, Veggies, Run!

It's night-time in the supermarket and the veggies are trying to keep fit! Use your stickers to complete the scene.

SNOW DAY

Just for fun

POO
POTATO

Page 15

Page 16-17 continued

13

Sticker Jigsaw

Supertato to the rescue! Use your stickers to complete the jigsaw.

Pineapple Panic!

Pineapple has climbed to the top shelf and now she's stuck!
Use your stickers to create some steps she can use to climb down.

Snow Day

It's a Snow Day in the supermarket.
Use your stickers to complete this wintry scene.

Stack the Shelves!

Oh no! The Evil Pea has made a huge mess in the supermarket!
Use your stickers to put the items back where they belong.

Create Your Own Super Veggie

Use this space to draw a Super Veggie of your own!
We've included an eye mask to get you started.

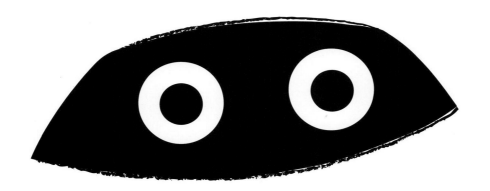

Dot-to-Dot

Join the dots to complete the image of the veggie!

Shopping Time!

Using your stickers, fill the trolley with the items on the shopping list.

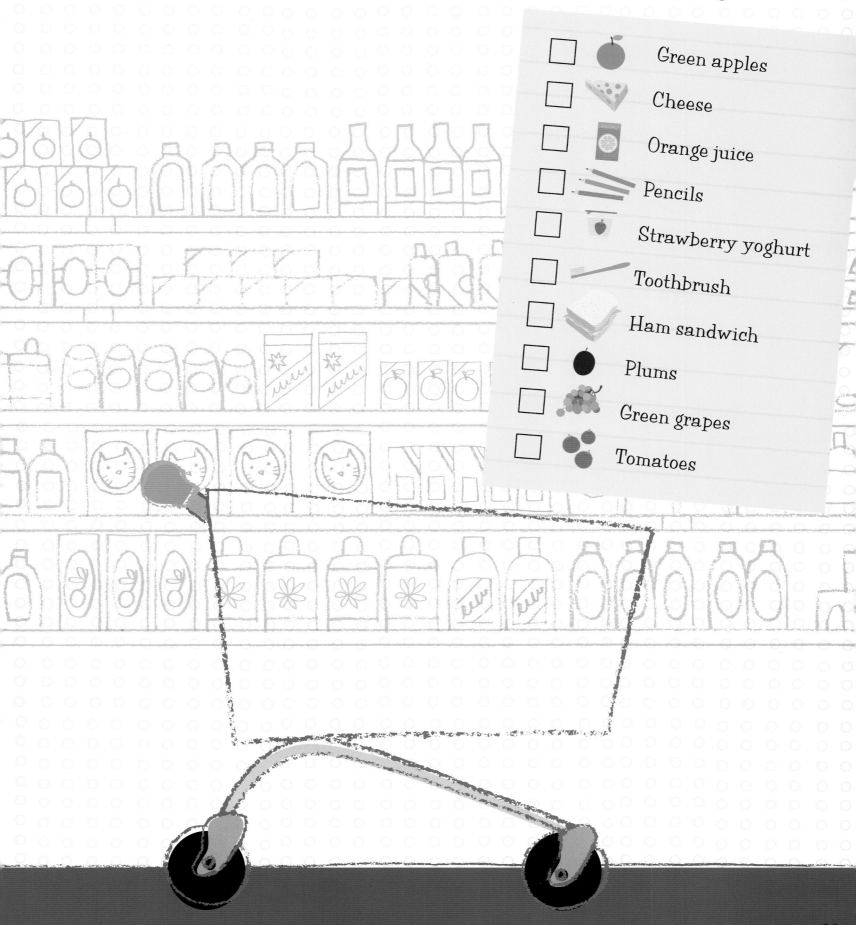

- ☐ Green apples
- ☐ Cheese
- ☐ Orange juice
- ☐ Pencils
- ☐ Strawberry yoghurt
- ☐ Toothbrush
- ☐ Ham sandwich
- ☐ Plums
- ☐ Green grapes
- ☐ Tomatoes

Party Set-Up

It's finally the day of the Carnival!
Use your stickers to help the veggies decorate the supermarket.

Bedtime

Shh! It's time for the veggies to go to sleep.
Use your stickers to help tuck them in with their teddy bears.